W9-ACA-975

International Standard Book Number:
0-926517-08-2

Library of Congress Catalog Card Number:
89-81984

© 1989 The Association of Performing Arts Presenters

The Association of Performing Arts Presenters
1112 16th Street, NW, Suite 620
Washington, DC 20036

Designed by Wickham & Associates, Inc.

An American Dialogue

THE NATIONAL TASK FORCE
ON PRESENTING AND TOURING
THE PERFORMING ARTS

Convened by The Rockefeller Foundation
The Pew Charitable Trusts
The National Endowment for the Arts

Writers and Consultants for the Task Force: William Keens, Keens Company
Naomi Rhodes, Naomi Rhodes Associates

On behalf of all the members of the National Task Force on Presenting and Touring the Performing Arts, I express our appreciation to The Rockefeller Foundation, The Pew Charitable Trusts, and the National Endowment for the Arts for their vision in providing the resources to form the Task Force. These convenors — and most particularly Dr. Alberta Arthurs, John Killacky, and Peter Pennekamp — were among the first to recognize the potential of the presenting and touring field in addressing many of the complex issues that face the arts and culture in America. They also recognized that a process was needed that encouraged participation by a great number of people from different backgrounds if presenting and touring were to be effectively represented. This emphasis on inclusion demanded reserves of time and energy from everyone involved, but it has resulted in a body of ideas that are sure to be essential to our work throughout the 1990s and into the next century.

What we heard in Task Force meetings were concepts that often challenged established ways of thinking and ideas that encouraged us to believe that solutions to complex problems are possible. We also came to realize that solutions to problems had to be carefully crafted, because similar techniques, under different circumstances, do not always produce similar results. Many of us who regarded ourselves as "experts" in our fields soon understood that greater expertise and knowledge were needed than any one person possessed. Our personal perspectives were, by definition, narrow ones, though each became part of the mosaic of opinions, insights and experiences that comprised this ongoing dialogue. In the end, however, one member of the Task Force took exception to this document because it was felt that the concerns of "cultural presenters grounded in their communities" were not adequately addressed.

The issues discussed in the following pages are crucial to the future of the performing arts in the United States. We ask that the reader bring to his or her reading the same commitment to listening, thinking, speaking, and responding that participants brought to the Task

Force process itself. We realize that there are those who will feel they are "too busy" to read this entire document. Both they and our field may be the poorer as a result. But it would be impossible to present a neatly packaged summary of all the issues, ideas, and points of view represented here. As one Task Force member remarked, this document *is* the executive summary. Its length and format are what this exhaustive and immensely rich dialogue required.

We also hope that the reader will take this publication *as a whole*, treating it as a philosophical essay against which future efforts can be measured. There are no bulleted recommendations at the end, no final list of specific actions. Instead, every page offers at least one, and usually several, recommendations and actions in their proper context, and often these items resurface as they apply elsewhere.

In this report, as in our field, context is everything. This document, therefore, can best serve as a resource and guide in many aspects of presenting and touring — from the development of a mission statement to the formation of relationships between a presenting organization and local artists. In effect, what follows is a kind of road map, one that suggests the directions for travel, describes any number of departure points, recognizes many destinations, and encourages a variety of routes.

This American dialogue has just begun. The process initiated by the convenors will continue far into the future as responses are developed to this document and as more of us in the field talk to one another about who we are, what we do, how we function, and why.

On behalf of the Task Force and the convenors, I wish to thank our consultants and the writers of this document, Naomi Rhodes and William Keens. They listened intently to over 125 thinkers and speakers, they gave written form to our ideas, and they succeeded in incorporating a great many of our voices and perspectives. The result is that this document is far greater than the sum of its parts.

The Association of Performing Arts Presenters, and particularly Executive Director Susan Farr, were also crucial in the success of our effort. They made certain that the process was effectively managed, that every element was executed on time, and that the concerns and perspectives of a great many constituencies were fully incorporated at every step of the way.

Lastly, I wish to express my personal and sincere appreciation to each of the individuals who served as members of the National Task Force on Presenting and Touring the Performing Arts. Their participation, ideas, energy, experience, passion, and clarity served as building blocks for the entire process, and will undoubtedly continue to serve the field well.

GERALD D. YOSHITOMI
Chair
The National Task Force
on Presenting and Touring the Performing Arts
November 1, 1989

INTRODUCTION

Presenters and touring artists have often been at
the forefront of the performing arts, offering work not
otherwise available and reaching diverse audiences and
changing communities. In a period of great demographic
and cultural flux, it is even more essential that audiences
and communities have access to the finest, most varied
arts experiences, and that artists reach the broadest public
in turn. The fullest development of our society is served if
we use presenting and touring both to respond to change
and be agents of it.

The National Task Force on Presenting and Touring the Performing Arts was convened to envision the
future of our field and build a philosophical framework for
action. It was created, and this document written, because
the need to examine who we are and what we do as a field
has become too compelling to postpone. At risk is the
force, content, and relevance of presenting and touring if
we do not place them in the broadest artistic, social,
cultural, and structural contexts. To achieve these objectives, we must do more than dream. We are called to urgent
activism.

Art of the highest quality can be created and
supported wherever people have an interest in it. This is
being demonstrated in small towns and medium-sized
cities as distant from one another as Whitesburg, Kentucky;
San Juan Bautista, California; Santa Fe, New Mexico;
Salina, Kansas; Portland, Maine; and Charleston, South
Carolina. Yet only in the last two decades have we begun
to recognize the breadth of genres, styles, sources, venues,
artists, artforms, and expressions that comprise the
performing arts and on which the future of presenting and
touring must be predicated. This is in contrast to the
established routine that presenting and touring followed
for many years, as art was given the stamp of approval in
New York and Europe before being disseminated elsewhere.

The convenors of the Task Force — The Rockefeller
Foundation, The Pew Charitable Trusts, and the National
Endowment for the Arts — recognized that a special
dialogue was needed to embrace this breadth of activity. In

the largest, most comprehensive, and most diverse national forum of its kind, more than 125 presenters, artists,
managers, funders, and representatives of state and local
arts agencies and regional organizations assembled in
small groups for eight meetings in various locations around
the country. Fourteen members of the Task Force also
served on a steering committee that met five times to
guide this process. Discussions were further informed by
ten commissioned "perspective papers" that drew on the
expertise of people both within and outside the Task Force.

This elaborate, eighteen-month undertaking,
which began in July 1988, created an expanding network
of communication among people and organizations representing diverse artforms and a range of cultural, racial,
and aesthetic perspectives. Because the composition of the
Task Force proved to be as varied as our field, many people
— both within and outside the group — became newly
aware of one another. Some of the bonds they formed have
already produced opportunities for additional discussions,
collaborations, projects, programs, and works of art.

These ties resulted from candid discussions about
difficult issues, some of which were given a public forum
for the first time. Consensus was not the first objective,
though it did occur at important moments. More often,
people recognized the value of their differences and the
strength that presenting derives from a large pool of
interests, convictions, and experiences. As Task Force
members read and responded to successive drafts of this
report, they were better able to focus their thinking and to
influence the views of their colleagues. In a field that is
finally learning to see itself *as* a field, that is newly
asserting itself as an artistic and economic force, it bodes
well that so many viewpoints shaped this process and that
genuine discourse was the result.

The primary audience for this report are those
people directly involved in presenting and touring. This is
where productive change and the opportunities it fosters
must be pursued: with presenters and their boards, advi-
sory groups, and staff; artists and their representative
organizations; artist managers; and the local, state, and

regional arts agencies, support organizations, and funders who understand the needs and potential of presenting and touring.

The extended audience is also part of our more broadly defined field. It includes educators, legislators, university administrators, city council members, and others whose actions and policies have a direct impact on what we do.

Before we can achieve the future envisioned in this report, we must acknowledge our interdependence and the new possibilities it creates. The field of presenting and touring must be bound by a mutuality of purpose which recognizes that our fates are joined and that our success or failure must be shared. No artist, presenter, or manager works alone. No audience and community experience art without the collaborative efforts of artists and arts organizations. No successful presenting occurs without the community as context.

For mutuality of purpose to be realized, presenting must be seen as a series of relationships, developed over time, that encourage exploration, experimentation, and trust. Audiences can come to know the work of an artist through repeated exposure. A presenter can learn more about artists and disciplines through ongoing communication with artists and managers. Artists can find more effective ways to reach their communities. The result will be the best work, presented under the best circumstances, for audiences that are fully engaged. This may well be the most enduring legacy of the Task Force and the most dramatic prelude to change.

1 THE HISTORICAL CONTEXT

This brief chapter is not an attempt to create a definitive history of presenting and touring the performing arts. That study, filled with the insight, detail, and anecdote it deserves, should someday be written. For the purpose of this report, it must be sufficient to touch briefly on a few of the influences that have shaped our profession as we know it in the United States.

The chief value of this historical context is in its reinforcement that *many* histories, cultures, and expressions comprise presenting and touring at their fullest. Experiencing all of them gives us a truer picture of both American and world cultures and contributes greatly to our artistic understanding and wealth. Thus, the most compelling reasons for the discussions of equity and diversity that occur throughout this essay are artistic and cultural ones.

Presenting the performing arts has been considered a profession only relatively recently. But the first "presenters" were probably those individuals or groups who developed performances for members of a definable community or made it possible for others to do so. In the earliest societies, such events might have included rites, rituals, ceremonies, and the telling of stories relating to hunting, fertility, initiation, changes in the weather, and so forth. A connection across time can be inferred between those societies and the immigrants from virtually every country in the world who brought with them to America the objects, ceremonies, and arts of their homelands. Facing hardship and often hostility, they found cohesiveness in the continuity of their cultures.

Though the history of the United States is largely one of immigration — both forced and voluntary — we must remember that numerous Native American civilizations were thriving on the North American continent before the arrival of settlers from other countries. For them, cultural survival has been a struggle against overwhelming odds for as long as four centuries. For African Americans, too, cultural survival has meant holding onto their heritage despite efforts over the centuries to divest them of it. Their music, writings, stories, dress, speech, religions, beliefs, and values are essential to their identity as a people and a vital part of the American experience. The same is true of the many Latino cultures, whose growing influence dates from the earliest European settlements and from Spanish domination of what is now the western United States. The strong traditions and ancient heritages of Asian Americans, whose labor first helped build America's railways, have also shaped our country.

Many of these cultures and people have been scarred by centuries of violence against them. Their traditions are lost or in jeopardy, and their communities have been subjected to exile and economic deprivation. The Task Force has acknowledged that many cultural experiences are rooted in pain as well as pride and hope. These histories, and the images and expressions that have grown from them, must be recognized and supported.

European immigration from the seventeenth through the early twentieth centuries was accompanied by territorial expansion and the fanning out of populations across the country. The Industrial Revolution of the nineteenth century, the linking of the country by rail, and the invention of the internal combustion engine all launched a period of unparalleled growth and mobility. The result was that communities could more easily make contact with one another, both through trade and by sharing their artistic talent. The saloon-based musicale, the circus, and the earliest forms of vaudeville, to name only a few, thrived during this period, and audiences across the country enjoyed performances that previously could only be seen in the large port cities.

A series of cultural movements in the nineteenth century contributed to an increasingly more active involvement with the arts in rural America. The Lyceum and Lyceum Speaker's Bureaus were aimed at the self-improvement of members through exposure to lectures by touring writers, philosophers, and scientists. The Chautauqua and the Tent Chautauqua Circuit brought theatre and other touring arts events to many communities. Later the Chautauqua developed into the Community Theatre movement, which encouraged a shift from interested spectator to active participant.

Those immigrants who arrived before 1924, when immigration laws became more restrictive, developed resources that enabled them to retain and share their cultural expressions. Although many artists were of exceptional ability, presentations were typically not "professional" in that they were not the artists' sole source of support. They often consisted of events staged by Irish, Italian, Chinese, Latino, or Jewish cultural organizations in private homes, churches, or community centers. Similar activities had been held, albeit surreptitiously, by members of African American communities since the advent of slavery. All of these events were the forerunners of many of the institutions that have since developed wherever audiences exist, and they continue to play an important role in virtually all cultural communities today.

From the mid-twenties until the early fifties, mostly as a result of the devastation of war and persecution in eastern and western Europe, immigrants who came to the United States sparked two developments. First, European immigrant artists, in response to the need to perform, contributed substantially to the producing organizations based on the European model. Second, the general population of European immigrants brought with them their hunger and demand for European-style performing arts events, which defined how presenting would be viewed for many years to come by a particular sector of the arts and presenting field.

Thus, the growth of interest in, and audiences for, European-derived artforms and artworks has its roots in the same kind of local "ethnic" activities that we see today among newer immigrants, many of whom arrived with the relaxation of immigration restrictions in the mid-fifties and again in the mid-seventies.

From South and Central America, Southeast Asia, Africa, the Caribbean, and throughout the world, new strands, colors, and patterns have been woven into the cloth of American culture. European immigrants, like others after them, understood that their arts and language were vital in defining who they were. Performing arts societies and "friends of..." groups were established to promote the expressions of their cultures. Much of our early chamber music touring, for example, came about as a result of commitments to support musicians who could give this artform expression. Many of the organizations that were created began as volunteer enterprises and remain so today. Symphony orchestras were established, often against great odds, because European immigrant communities knew that these institutions signaled the presence of their cultures. Even where no presenters or adequate facilities existed, there were potential audiences. Word of mouth and ads placed in local foreign-language newspapers by impresarios like the legendary Sol Hurok generated attendance at event after event in far-flung towns and cities.

This history of changing demographics, new waves of immigrants, and the nurturing of cultural traditions and artistic expressions has also been played out on the academic stage. As American colleges and universities grew in size, number, and stature, it was accepted that art and culture were an important part of a liberal arts education. Faculty members often invited professional artists to perform on campuses, both to support their teaching and to enrich their students' educational experience. As more colleges and universities built performing arts facilities, their presenting functions grew. Other faculty members took on additional responsibilities, and staff was added to manage these operations. By the late 1960s, a full-fledged touring market existed, stimulating the audience demand for more.

But the 2,000-seat halls constructed on many campuses, and in cities across the country, to accommodate big, European-style events such as symphony orchestras and ballet companies, often proved inappropriate for performances that require a more intimate setting. Presenters in these facilities were frequently uninterested in anything other than what they already knew or felt would be financially viable. Alternative spaces, created and controlled by artists, developed in reaction to this situation and have functioned for almost three decades as places for the new, contemporary, and unfamiliar.

In presenting and touring, as in the United States as a whole, demographic and cultural change is always taking place, new expressions, artists, and audiences are always emerging, and the field of presenting is always in flux. As more people regard it as their right to be able to see performances that reflect their cultures, issues of access and equity become more pressing. In addition, for purposes of a fuller cultural understanding, all Americans deserve access to the broader range of cultures in our country. Our response must be a greater commitment on the part of presenters and funders to encourage more touring by artists, ensembles, and companies from a wide range of backgrounds.

Even as new facilities and arts institutions are being built to provide this access, however, they are frequently out of step with changing local communities and cultural change. In Miami and Los Angeles, in New Orleans, Chicago, New York and Seattle, and in numerous places in between — including rural and small communities — many artists, artforms, and traditions are still denied adequate recognition, support, and access to stages on which to perform.

For reasons that must be apparent, this report could never be a fixed snapshot in time. It is, instead, an argument for the recognition that "culture," "art," "artist," "audience," "community," "presenting," and "touring" are living words that convey motion and discovery. It is meant to help the reader anticipate, not just react. History may not be a predictor of the future, but it is at least a prelude in which the themes of the future are sounded. In the United States at the beginning of the twenty-first century, the themes are diversity and change.

Activism and presenting must be more than silent partners. Fortunately, presenters are well suited to meet the challenges that change brings. Presenting organizations tend to be lean operations with low overhead and small administrative structures, existing to discover and stage the next artist or artwork, and doing so many times in the course of a season. Because a presenter is not necessarily limited to one particular artform, a variety of artists, styles, and cultures can be expressed.

Still, there are problems. Funding for most non-European-derived and contemporary art activities is far from equitable, and the infrastructure for the support of presenting organizations and artists is not what it should be. Many fundamental issues, such as having access to the best and most diverse work regardless of where one lives, have not been fully addressed. And the needs of touring artists are regarded as an afterthought by too many presenters and funders.

The Task Force saw evidence of the potential to address these problems and, increasingly, a willingness to take on that challenge. Presenting is more than a delivery system, after all, and presenters are more than just agents of distribution. Presenting encompasses all the performing arts, from every period, in every conceivable style, form, and setting. It entails understanding the complexity of the arts and our communities, dealing with unfamiliar artists and expressions before they are widely accepted, reaching those whom others may overlook, and expanding the concept of community to embrace more than audience alone. This points to a much more complete description of what presenters do than has commonly been recognized.

Function, not form, determines who is a presenter. Our field is strong because of the variety within it, including independent, nonprofit presenting organizations, festivals, presenters who work within "host" institutions such as universities or municipal governments, performing arts centers, museums, galleries, community centers, social service organizations, churches, and nightclubs. Also included are presenters who can be recognized by the type of work they present, such as contemporary or alternative arts centers, chamber music societies, jazz clubs, and organizations that present work from a specific culture. Performing arts producing organizations — such as dance companies, symphonies, or theatres — when they present other companies, are equally part of our field.

Presenting organizations operate in isolated communities as well as urban areas. Presenters work in old and new facilities and in renovated spaces, in art centers built to revitalize downtowns, in suburban neighborhoods and rural areas. Complexes of major halls, alternative spaces, and facilities designed for other primary uses may house presenting organizations.

Within any of these categories, further distinctions are possible. Festivals that celebrate the arts include community street fairs and international events. Colleges that house presenting organizations may range from a community college in the Southwest with responsibility for an area as large as Massachusetts, to a city university branch whose audience is a densely populated neighborhood.

All of these presenting organizations have much more in common than they have differences. Issues of artistic integrity and representation, of access and programming, of audience development and marketing, of mission, funding and governance — these are important to virtually every presenter. To define our field inclusively, we must recognize these commonalities and look beyond the superficial distinctions that separate us. Narrow definitions, sometimes in response to equally narrow funding criteria, can divide rather than unify us. We must nurture and encourage good presenters even if they do not fit some predetermined "norm."

The Task Force recognized that the best activist presenters have a strong understanding of, and experience with, a wide variety of artforms, artists, and cultural contexts, enabling these presenters to function as knowledgeable curators of the art and artists on their stages. They also take the initiative in effectively and appropriately marketing artists and their work, making the community an integral part of what they do, educating new audiences and creating a welcoming atmosphere for them, building long-term relationships with artists, articulating their organizations' purposes, and responsibly managing resources, staffs, and facilities.

In short, where artistic vision, artistic engagement, and a strong relationship with community exist within a well-run and tightly managed organization, the presenter can create an environment in which art and artists flourish and communities are well served.

Artistic vision asserts a particular point of view, a knowledge of and instinct for the artists and artwork being presented, a genuine interest in the art itself, and the determination to see that artists and their art reach the public. As it drives the presenting organization, it influences what is performed and what context is created, how audiences are educated and prepared, and what relationship the artwork has to other pieces that have been or will be presented. Without the content-based programming that artistic vision implies, presenting loses its meaning.

When a presenter asserts this artistic vision, he or she is acting on the same responsibilities that a museum curator exercises in selecting work for exhibition. This might entail exploring new ground, creating a basis for understanding other works in the exhibition or future exhibitions, recognizing young talent, challenging the local audience, recalling the past, addressing the present, or describing the future. This curatorial function in the selection of a season is at the core of the presenter's role.

Nor is artistic vision the province of any one type of presenter. Whether the presenter programs work that is classical or avant garde, single- or multi-disciplinary, traditional or contemporary, or specifically rooted in a particular culture, good presenting must be driven by artistic vision.

Artistic engagement describes the strong relationship that must exist between presenters and the artists and artworks they present. This is more than optional. An element of necessity characterizes inspired presenting: the need to experience the art directly; to know, communicate with, and help support artists; and to share this passion with audiences.

An active, ongoing relationship with artists is often the source of artistic engagement, becoming the lifeblood of a presenting organization and contributing powerfully to the performance experience. Composer and performer Paul Dresher has seen it pay off: "As an artist who tours, these are our most satisfying engagements — with presenters who acknowledge a continuity of relationship." Artistic engagement also acknowledges that artists must be respected and sustained over time if our field is to have the best benefit of their expression.

Presenters and presenting organizations are in a good position to provide this ongoing support to artists. They can give artists rehearsal and studio space in facilities and access to technical equipment. In addition to paying artists' fees, they can commission new works, revive classics, share artistic treasures with audiences, and make multi-year commitments to creation and production. They can introduce artists to the media, offer promotion and marketing support, supply administrative structure and guidance, and connect artists to other presenters and presenting organizations.

The interaction of a strong artist-presenter relationship describes a mutuality of purpose that must characterize our business attitudes and dealings. Artists and presenters often see themselves as adversaries in this arena, and the creative possibilities go unexplored. Creating and presenting performances of the highest quality should be the first point of discussion as presenters, artists, and their managers develop projects, residencies, tours, and commissions. Contracts and fees alone are not what keep us together; without a strong artist-presenter relationship they can just as easily divide us.

Rebecca Lewis, in her perspective paper, "The Perfect Presenter," captured this when she recounted what artists told her they look for in a presenter:

> In sum, the most beloved presenters are those who exhibit a personal passion for experiencing artists'

work and who can convey an institutional enthusi-
asm for the works being presented. These presenters
will most likely:
- *take the trouble to know something of the artwork*
  and the artist;
- *be knowledgeable of and sensitive to the needs of*
  his or her own community;
- *work imaginatively to get the audience to the*
  theatre;
- *provide stress reduction for the traveling artist (a*
  few amenities will usually do);
- *see that any non-performance activities are well-*
  integrated and well-planned;
- *understand their own role as educators within the*
  community.

Strong relationship with community requires the development of an ongoing dialogue between presenters and their communities, both about the art and artists and about the context for their presentation. It requires activism on the part of the presenter, a commitment to the interaction of artist and audience, and the recognition that community is more than audience alone.

Achieving this relationship is encouraged by incorporating the community into all aspects of the presenting organization's activities and decision making, which in turn generates community support. So integral is this to the act of presenting that many Task Force members easily regarded community as the true source of all culture and the most sustaining context for the presentation of both art and artists.

Internal Support Structures

Whether they operate within host institutions, such as a city government or university, or as independent entities, all presenting organizations depend upon internal support structures to help them pursue their missions. These structures facilitate the daily operations of the presenting organization. They include, for example, form of governance, type of organization, staff and board, mission statement, volunteers, relationships among departments, and much more. The value of these structures, and one indicator of their effectiveness, is the extent to which they help establish the balance between artistic independence and organizational stability.

Activism in presenting and the possibility of programmatic and financial "failure" are not strangers to one another. Precisely because failure is the outcome that we often fear most, support structures must anticipate its likelihood and build a buffer against it if the presenting organization is to control its own fate. We can begin to do this by redefining both "success" and "failure" in terms of the missions and objectives of our organizations, rather than solely in financial terms.

For example, if artistic venturesomeness is embraced in the mission statement and pursued through managerial policy, an organization is better equipped to take advantage of opportunities that might otherwise paralyze it. Often such a mission statement is developed in consultation with community representatives, host institution administrators, boards of directors, local artists, and others. From this, reasonable goals and objectives can be developed. A strong mission statement enables an organization to evaluate itself over time, not just on the basis of a single performance or season, and to explain itself clearly to funders and others.

The idea of linking support structures to artistic risk is still not widely practiced in our field. For any organization, risk entails making commitments to artists, works of art, audiences, and sometimes controversial issues, then treating these commitments as seriously as fundraising goals. Where board and staff understand this, they are best equipped to incorporate "risk management" into the fabric of their organization.

It is ironic that presenters in organizations with the most opportunity for stability, such as those that are part of a larger host institution, are sometimes the least inclined to explore their artistic leeway. In effect, too *much* stability may be a conservative influence that a presenter should balance by giving extra attention to artistic leadership. Conversely, organizations that are disposed to take artistic risks may need to concentrate on the development of a board of directors and a secure funding base in order to become more stable, enabling continued risk-taking.

For a presenting organization that operates within a host institution, stability and solvency may be assured, but the presenting organization may be overshadowed by the host because of conflicting goals. Further, the presenter may be answerable to people who have little idea what the organization does or why it does it. The presenter typically lacks control over the actions of these higher authorities, such as the trustees of a major university or city council members.

Here, too, a clear, specific mission statement is vital. Mission statements that are built on an assessment of who the constituency is, what its needs are, what is being presented or produced elsewhere, and the purpose for which the organization exists will best support the individual decisions made by presenters. Such a statement places the presenting organization's mission in the context of the host institution's broader objectives and provides a framework within which the presenter can operate. But this is a two-way street: those higher authorities also have an obligation to learn what the presenting organization needs and then to help provide for those needs.

The entire staff of a presenting organization represents another important component of the internal support structure. Staff must be valued and trained so that their skills match their responsibilities and so that they understand fully the work of the organization. In addition, job descriptions and objectives should be clearly linked to the organization's mission statement. The lack of staff development ultimately damages any presenting organization's effectiveness. Staff dissatisfaction and turnover are increasingly cause for concern, since our field can ill afford such losses just as it is taking on more cultural responsibilities and more demanding projects. Many presenting organizations continue to offer wages and benefits that are too meager to attract and retain talented individuals who can meet these challenges.

In rural and small communities, where resources, staff, and volunteers are usually stretched to the limit, burnout is a particular problem. Volunteers are often relied upon to do the work of paid staff; where staff does exist, it is usually a single person trying to do the work of several. Evaluation in these and all other organizations must take working conditions, stress, and burnout into account. And all staff must be measured against standards that are appropriate to the mission of the organization.

What about the board of directors? There are multiple views as to how best to develop, constitute, utilize, and incorporate a board, depending upon the nature of the organization, its purpose, and the environment in which it operates. For many organizations, the traditional non-profit board of community and business leaders who take an active role in governance and policy development, and who give and raise money, is most effective in building and sustaining an institution.

One alternative is described by George Thorn in his perspective paper, "The Role of the Board In a Rapidly Changing Society." Thorn argues for rethinking the institution of the board of directors to make it more suited to the changing environment. Instead of a bigger-is-better approach to board development, for example, he recommends a minimum number of directors, perhaps three or four, but no more than is set by state law. Then, as needed

> *all other expertise, services, and support should be supplied by task forces, individuals, and committees of volunteers who surround the staff and board. Bridges and relationships would be developed between these satellites and the appropriate staff and/or board function. Community volunteers with limited time would thus be able to help the organization on a job-specific basis without requiring a commitment of them beyond their needs, abilities, or available time.*

Thorn describes this approach as "casting community partners." It is the most viable alternative, he says, to "the black hole of unending responsibility, work, guilt, little reward, and not much chance of success," that constitutes the board experience for many trustees.

For an organization that wants to establish as many links to as many communities as possible, another alternative might be very different from the one described by Thorn. Rather than being a small nucleus, the board might consist of a great many people, each of whom brings some particular relationship with community to the presenting organization.

Whatever its size and structure, the roles and composition of a board directly affect an organization's ability to carry out its mission. Further, that mission is shaped by the perspectives, counsel, and actions of the board. In whatever form, therefore, the board must be more than organizational window dressing. This is an especially sensitive matter as an organization attempts to respond to issues of cultural equity and board diversification. Robert Garfias, in his paper, "Cultural Diversity and the Arts in America," comments on efforts by arts organizations to build culturally diverse boards.

> The arts structure seeks these people out in an attempt to satisfy the need for diverse representation on the board or committee, rather than to seek diverse opinions. As a result, minorities are often chosen because their backgrounds match the expectations of those already in the structure rather than because they represent another point of view.

As George Thorn says, "In successful organizations, the working relationship [between board and staff] is always one of an active, dynamic, supportive, trusting, and equal partnership." The activism that must be the hallmark of presenting and touring can only be sustained if our internal support structures advance our commitment to renewal and change. Activism that is grounded in these structures stands the greatest chance of being sustained over a long period of time and of affecting all other aspects of a presenting organization's activities.

Every artist, even the most private, belongs to at least one community of some kind. This may be a community of artists engaged in the same discipline, a community of people exploring similar ideas, or a small community of family and friends. All belong to the community they call "home." In this way, every artist is a local artist somewhere. Touring, when it occurs, is the space and time that, ideally, provides the support and sustenance that enable the artist to create at home.

Artists live in every city. They also live in many rural and small communities where their art may be fed by quiet and solitude, by their love for the local culture, and by a strong communal commitment. Whatever the local setting, this is where they ruminate, create, practice, grow, and rehearse. It is also where they live, love, and grieve. For some, the home base is their first and most important audience. For others, it is principally the place from which they tour. For both, it supplies a powerful, indelible context for what they do.

Pianist Edwin Romain recalls that his relationship to the people and city of Charleston, South Carolina, encompassed many roles and responsibilities. Along with his duo-pianist partner, Wilfred Delphin, he is a national touring artist who performs locally and is a role model for aspiring artists. While in Charleston, he served as a presenter at Piccolo Spoleto and participated in planning sessions for the Spoleto Festival. He was a resource for area schools and the municipal and state arts councils, and served on the faculty of a university. And he performed with both out-of-town and local artists on many occasions.

Says Romain, "Local artists can be both those of the highest quality and those who are less accomplished. Both have a need to be nourished, and both are community resources. At issue is whether presenters and others recognize this value and try to advance this relationship."

Despite the bond of local artists to community, a bias often permeates the institutional attitude toward them — as if, at home, they are somehow less creative, less worthy, less professional. On the road, they may be widely acclaimed; when they come home, they are "just local." At the same time, many artists find themselves having to tour more than they might like because they won't be adequately supported or recognized at home until they are first accepted elsewhere.

For this reason, presenters, funders, and service organizations must provide sufficient support for local artists *before* they go on the road. Often that first local presentation provides an opportunity for work to be seen by audiences, as well as by other potential presenters. Support at home can also include making local facilities available for rehearsal and mounting productions to go on the road.

How important is a supportive home environment to artists? One indicator is the language we use to describe desirable situations for touring companies. We say that they have found "a second home" or established "a residency," terms that recreate in the touring environment something that is implicit at home. This includes having a certain command and control over their creative circumstances, often in ways as simple and direct as Merce Cunningham's idea of "keeping to a professional schedule." In the conversation between Cunningham and his company's executive director, Art Becofsky — which was the basis for Becofsky's perspective paper, "On Commissioning and Presenting New Art: From a Conversation with Merce Cunningham" — the two men speak of meshing artists' needs and community needs in a residency so that the "activities more resemble the things that artists do in their lives, rather than fabrications of what we think audiences might want to experience."

In effect, attitudes and practices developed in the home community become a touchstone for the artist on tour. The most productive engagements and residencies draw upon this home/road continuum to the benefit of all involved. For example, choreographer and dancer Liz Lerman has been working with older people for the past decade and has frequently been cited as an artist whose impact on this particular group has been very effective. Though her home base is Washington, D.C., she has a place anywhere an older person wants to learn to move.

The Roadside Theater offers another example of the far-reaching influence of "home." Based at Appalshop, an Appalachian cultural center in rural Whitesburg, Kentucky, Roadside stages plays whose source is the rich cultural legacy of the people in southeastern Kentucky and southwestern Virginia — the "mountain people." All of the performers in Roadside are themselves from that community. They are local artists who started from a point of particular engagement with community and who, when they go on tour, attempt to recreate that same interaction with other communities, whether they be in rural North Dakota or urban southern California.

Because artists are, by definition, creative activists and risk-takers, they can sometimes be instrumental in helping presenters both to anticipate and to determine how to work with changing communities. This concept is particularly important in presenting culturally diverse work or creating new ways of reaching communities.

On tour, artists will bring their view of community with them — one that may be very different from the presenter's. This difference should be respected. Artists may have ideas about interacting with a presenter's communities which the presenter may never have considered. Artists may know of people locally who could assist in building interest in a performance. Some of these ideas may be workable, others may not; artists and presenters must sort them out together. But whether at home or on tour, local artists represent a resource that our field cannot afford to squander. To do so would be a serious loss to ourselves and to the public with whom artists and presenters interact.

4 THE LOCAL ENVIRONMENT

To say that presenting demands a strong relationship with "community" is to use that term deliberately. "Audience" is simply too limiting to describe the array of people, beyond our valued ticket-buyers, whom presenters and artists must engage. Community implies a fundamental social partnership that makes presenting and touring both complete and compelling.

Community

Community is approachable in many ways. A presenter may think of community one way when programming the entire canon of Schubert's work, another when presenting the Bunraku Theatre, and a third when seeking family audiences for weekend performances of the dance company Forces of Nature. These approaches to community are not mutually exclusive, yet considering them separately allows us to understand better the relationships between presenters and community members.

Community as culturally defined refers to a group of people, larger than the audience alone, who share a common heritage. A community might be African Americans from the Caribbean or mountain people in Appalachia. The distinguishing feature is not race; nor is community necessarily geographically bounded. What holds it together are shared cultural experiences so strong that the community is the well-spring for, and the renewer of, the work of the presenter, who is necessarily a member of that community.

Community as artistically defined recognizes that individuals are often drawn together to experience, learn about the work of, and support certain artists and works of art. They might include devotees of particular artists or of a particular discipline or genre. Though this community is often expressed as ticket-buyers, it is not limited to audience alone, since the influence of artists and art works may reach beyond the box office.

Community as defined by geography and market usually refers to those who have purchased or may purchase tickets to a performing arts event. This includes discrete groups, such as senior citizens and families, or a neighborhood in close proximity to a presenting organization. Community in this instance is often bounded geographically, and although it is larger than the audience, it is frequently expressed as the potential for the public to become ticket-buyers.

Presenters who have a sure grasp of their communities and of where they stand in relation to them are well served by their understanding: they know how the arts are experienced; their roles as presenters are sharper; they are equipped to influence and help lead their communities; and the artistic missions of their organizations are sensitive and clear.

Presenters must be actively and visibly engaged in their communities, working with (and sometimes against, if necessary) other community leaders and spokespersons to articulate diverse community needs, interests, and standards. On matters of censorship, presenters must be as vocal as those who would limit artistic expression. By making serious issues public, presenters can help ensure that those issues are openly debated and that artists and presenters alike are participants in those debates.

Caron Atlas offers a perspective on the presenter-community relationship in her paper, "Culture and Community":

- *The relationship is a collaborative process, with culture growing from the community and feeding the community.*
- *Built on mutual respect, mutual trust and mutual change, the relationship is about more than art. Cultural, social, economic, and political life are deeply interconnected....Culture isn't imposed on the community, it is owned by the community.*
- *There is a strong commitment made over a long period of time.*

Local artists are one important component in the communities with whom presenters interact. Frequently, in rural and small communities, local artists create work

that is an outgrowth of their community's indigenous
life. In many regions of the country, in these small
communities live artists of color whose work is overlooked. Supporting local artists creates a tone of respect
for their work and publicly acknowledges their value to
society at large. From this, trust, understanding and mutual
commitment can grow.

Local artists are often at a disadvantage in dealing
with presenters, however, especially when funding guidelines exclude support for presentation within a company's home city or state. Needless to say, such guidelines
do little to promote long-term artist-presenter relationships. Fortunately, more presenters are collaborating with
local artists, developing performance opportunities for
them, and creating work-related interactions with artists
on tour.

Caron Atlas describes how the Roadside Theater,
which places a high value on interaction with local communities and artists, approaches touring as a form of
cultural exchange.

> Says Dudley Cocke, director of Roadside Theater,
> which tours regularly, "A key thing is for both the
> company and the presenter to define the purpose of
> the visit before it happens. We exchange information
> about our respective communities and talk about our
> respective long-range goals. How will our brief visit
> advance these goals? What large patterns is the
> event part of?"
> In the fall of 1988, Roadside toured North Dakota
> for a month. The heart of the tour was the goal of
> highlighting the local cultures of rural North Dakota
> communities. Roadside shared the stage at each stop
> with Native American dancers, cowboy poets,
> Acadian string bands, and other local artists, and
> reinforced the message that communities must listen
> to their own stories.

Presenters and local artists can work together in
other ways as well. Artists from one's home community

can be informed advisors to a presenting organization about other artists and artistic developments. As board members, artists can be community advocates and can voice artistic concerns. Presenters, in turn, can support local artists by advocating on their behalf in the local political system and familiarizing other presenters with their work. And when making presenting and commissioning decisions, presenters can consider the work of local artists.

For presenters, the commitment to community also entails exploring as wide a range of artistic expressions as possible, joining artists at the forefront of cultural development and renewal in our society. Supporting artists in the development of new works and ways of working is part of this responsibility, even though the results may be controversial. Euripedes, Shakespeare, Valdez, Brecht, Nijinsky, Graham, Shange, Wagner, Utamaro, and Thelonious Monk all created works that, at their premieres, were controversial. Those same works are now considered among the finest examples of their artforms. In allowing for and accepting the occasional controversy, presenters help insure that future generations and communities are artistically engaged and culturally tolerant.

Presenters and Their Relationships to Communities

The three definitions of community cited above are only a few examples of ways to view community. Rather than being a static concept, "community" embraces the widest range of interpretations and is limited only by the presenter's reach and imagination. When we speak of presenting in relation to community, we begin to imply where the partners stand in this collaborative process and how they interact with their local environments. Here, too, the discussions of the Task Force revealed several points of view.

One view might be described as essentially spherical in concept: artists, managers, presenters, community, funders, and audience are located around the surface of a sphere, without hierarchy or sequence in their relationship. At any time, any partner in the presenting process can interact with any other, and ideas may originate at any point and move in any direction. This idea stresses the inter-reliance of *everyone* in accomplishing something bigger than *anyone*.

Another view considers the relationships in a circular fashion. The artist appears in the center, while all other players are in service to the artist. The relationships are interactive, both around the circle and from the circumference to the center, but the structure exists primarily to support the artist and the creation of art.

Finally, a third view perceives art itself — rather than presenters, artists, and so forth — in relationship to other elements in a cultural ecosystem. These elements include cultural values, science, history, religion, law, and many other expressions of our humanity. Presenters, artists, and funders are actors within this ecosystem, and art both projects and reflects its cultural source. What is of primary importance in this view is the survival of the culture, not of a particular artist or artistic event. This global view proves particularly useful as we turn to the question of what constitutes American culture and to related issues of cultural equity. It underscores the point that what some people have considered the complete canon of artists, artforms, and disciplines is, in fact, only a small part of the whole range of a presenter's possibilities.

All of these perspectives are valid. They clarify the kind of relationship presenters may achieve with both the community and other partners in the presenting process, they point to the art that may result, and they suggest how funders and other organizations can assist in presenting, and touring that art.

Audience

Audiences attend performances for many reasons, in addition to their curiosity about the art being presented. They may come out of a commitment to, and love for, a particular kind of work or a particular artist. They may come to escape routine and seek social interaction,

wanting to be part of a group that experiences a live performance. They may come to educate themselves or their
children. They may come because they are interested in
the subject or content of a work. And they may come
because the presenting organization offers work that
springs from and reaffirms their cultural experiences and
traditions.

Encouraging audiences to attend a performance,
maintaining their involvement, and challenging them
are vital to the presenter's relationship with community.
At each step the presenter faces considerations of how the
art is described, of the artist-audience relationship, and of
the needs and interests of the audience — in a word, marketing. Neill Archer Roan, in his perspective paper "Marketing in the Next Decade," acknowledges the scope of
this challenge.

> *Marketing directors of the nineties must create*
> *identities for their organizations that powerfully*
> *underscore the value of the presenting organization*
> *to its communities and to the arts.*

Roan observes that because of changing demographics, "markets are not only segmented, they are frac-
tionalized." As the cost of advertising to these multiple
markets goes up, "word-of-mouth marketing" and "direct
sales methods" will become more attractive and more
effective.

> *All the highfalutin market research techniques,*
> *algorithmic factor-weighting formulas, psychogra-*
> *phic segmentation methodologies, and high-priced*
> *computer applications in the world will never equal*
> *the relationship opportunities, person-to-person*
> *communications, and sense of community that exist*
> *naturally in a grass roots community — be it small*
> *town, urban neighborhood, or rural valley. There's*
> *no marketing or advertising technique anywhere that*
> *can build audiences and enlist support for the arts*
> *like an enthusiastic community member talking up*

last night's performance over a drug store
counter....Marketing at the grass roots level is about
people talking to one another, building community
together, sharing and creating vision together, and
reaping their reward together.

When, as a result of these marketing efforts, audiences become more responsive to the artwork being presented, their responsiveness helps establish a connection
with the artists. Artists and audiences thus share a level of
creativity that is activated by work in which both have a
stake. Part of the artist's responsibility is to create the
fullest context for this experience. For their part, presenters must encourage exchanges with artists who are interested and effective communicators. Presenters should also
recognize that time spent in these activities by artists is
additional time, which must be scheduled in advance
and for which they must be compensated.

The development and maintenance of commit-
ted audiences depends also on the availability of informed,
high-quality cultural journalism and arts criticism. Too
often, newspapers and other media treat performing arts
events with no sense of their importance. They do not
investigate or enlighten in their coverage, and the assigned
writer is often unfamiliar with the artform and artists.
This lack of readiness is most evident in feature articles or
reviews dealing with new work, work of artists of color,
and work that is not part of the European canon. Throughout the country, the Task Force heard repeatedly of long-
standing patterns of such neglect by the media, and of
biases against artists of color, alternative venues, and new
or unfamiliar works.

Audiences and artists have the right to expect the
performing arts to be intelligently covered in their local
and national media. Presenters can encourage this by
staying in constant, friendly, and supportive contact with
thoughtful arts writers and critics. One presenter, for
example, spoke about how he supplies the music critic of
the local daily with a weekly tape of selections from a
variety of world musics, with which the critic must be

familiar in order to write about the wide range of musical performances in their city.

Encouraging informed cultural journalism is an important activist role for presenters. This might also be accomplished by involving writers in non-writer roles, such as inviting them to speak about a program or artist if they have particular qualifications to do so. Presenters can also commission writers to do challenging pieces for program books, or newsletters and make them available prior to as well as at the performances. Chamber Music Chicago does this, sending detailed, carefully researched and well-written program notes to its subscribers ten days in advance of the concert so the audience will arrive at the performance better informed and fully-prepared for the event. A presenter might him or herself write from time to time for a local newspaper, or record commentary on the arts for a local radio station that may not have qualified journalists to cover the performing arts. Finally, a presenter might recommend and encourage the employment of broadly knowledgeable cultural journalists; at the same time, journalists without such knowledge should be expected to undertake the training and education needed to acquire it.

In some respects, good cultural journalism is an issue of equity — a matter of according artists and audiences everywhere a measure of respect. But equity in relation to audiences goes beyond recognizing and reviewing a wide range of artists and presentations. It also means seeking out, listening to, and following the best advice of those diverse cultural communities.

A presenter who has no relationship with his or her local cultural communities cannot program an isolated artist or event for those communities and expect an ongoing commitment from the audiences. Nor is a high level of commitment achieved through marketing sleight-of-hand. Diversified audiences are more than followers, and to diversify our audiences we must treat those communities as a significant source of what the presenting organization does. Their leadership must be involved in planning before programs are finalized. Community organizations should be compensated for the use of their mailing lists and expertise. Just as we pay professional marketers to bring in new audiences, we have the same obligation to the culturally specific organizations from whom we seek advice.

Cultural diversity in audiences may also be influenced by where an event is located. For example, some theatres that were long closed to African Americans remain uncomfortable places for them to attend performances because of that history, even if the artists performing are themselves of African descent. Creating a "sympathetic environment" requires that our field be sensitive to such matters, as well as to dress code, ticket pricing, whether children are welcome, and whether food is allowed in the hall. These policies can be changed on an event-by-event basis to serve particular audiences.

In his perspective paper, Robert Garfias underscores how much is at stake in creating sympathetic environments.

> ... our art institutions seem to say that 'you must belong here to enter' and 'you must know what you are doing here.' For these new immigrants and a good number of other diverse ethnic groups in America there is little or no incentive to meet this challenge. To them our open doors appear as tightly shut as ever. The apparent hostility of our arts institutions to the non-initiated is, most unfortunately, something vividly clear to those outside and at the same time something unimaginable to those working within the institutional network structure.

Where presenters succeed in involving communities in a meaningful way, and where the respect for them is evident, audiences will gather.

Education

To be a presenter is to embark on a life-long process of self-education, constantly striving to increase one's awareness and understanding of numerous artforms, disciplines, and artists, as well as of the dynamics of their communities. One of the most important ways to accomplish this is for presenters to see as many performances of the widest variety possible. Because of the imperative to see performances, presenting organizations must budget money for and support presenters who have to travel to other cities to see work. This need must be recognized by funders, service organizations, state arts agencies, and regional organizations as legitimate and deserving of funding.

The extent to which presenters can be effective educators in their communities is often the extent to which they are willing and able to engage in self-education. Keen interest, commitment, curiosity, and an activist's orientation are all essential.

The educational process works in many directions: from artists to presenters, who often lack an understanding of anything rooted in cultures other than their own, or arts disciplines other than those they already know; from artists and presenters to audiences, especially when audiences are being introduced to the richness of their own and other cultures or to an unfamiliar artist, expression or artform for the first time; from communities to artists and presenters, who depend upon a larger cultural context to complete what they do; from presenters to artists, who cannot be assumed to have a particular understanding of every presenter's mission and circumstances; and from artists, presenters, and communities to the funders and others who are more likely to support this educational process if they understand its value.

One of the most important responsibilities of presenters is to be educators. The first purpose of this education must be to expand the community's awareness of the sources and breadth of American art and culture.

There are many ways to approach the presentation of work from diverse cultures with attention to context, including fuller contextual notes in programs, pre- and post-performance discussions with artists, if appropriate, and educational programming designed for specific audiences. Improved media coverage and cultural journalism, increased scholarship related to the art and artists of diverse cultures, and more cross-cultural performance experiences represent opportunities as well. It is also as important for urban residents to experience the traditional arts that often flourish in rural and small communities as it is for people in those communities to see the work growing from urban experiences.

Perspective paper author Thomas Wolf in "The Presenter's Role In Education" suggests that presenting organizations cannot undertake the responsibilities of education alone. For this reason, partnerships must be developed "with colleges and universities, other arts organizations (including producing organizations), community music schools and dance academies, private schools, civic and fraternal organizations, and with other institutions that can contribute to a community-wide response to the challenge of arts education." In every community, pursuing these educational goals can be enhanced by making better use of the personnel, facilities, and resources of the established public and private education system, and by using artists and artist networks to help create sensitive educational environments.

One noteworthy presenting venture that has effectively utilized a city's resources in service to education is the Philadelphia International Children's Theatre Festival. A program of the University of Pennsylvania's Annenberg Center, the Festival has brought to the city international companies with original works written for children. As a part of the Festival, the Annenberg Center has created a major community-wide education program in partnership with local performing arts groups and the schools.

Education in the artistic expressions of diverse cultures must rest in the hands of people who are rooted in and understand those cultures. After all, ours is a field where no one can be an expert in everything, where by definition almost everything is in flux. The educational environment is especially fluid now, as Robert Garfias points out.

In a recent New York Times *article, a professor of humanities at the University of Virginia said, in response to the proposed new curriculum which has been expanded beyond Western civilization, "We know how to put things in the Western tradition in context, but most of us don't have the slightest idea what the contexts of Indian music, Japanese poetry and Indian philosophy are."*

Garfias stresses a crucial step that arts educators must take:

The arts need to be reintroduced — not merely talking about the arts and developing art appreciation, but "doing" art. One of the reasons that the arts are more generally valued, supported and participated in by the general population in Europe and Japan is that there has been, from the elementary school level, much more active participation in the performance and the execution of the arts. Upon such a basis one can later intellectualize. Without the basis of first-hand practical experience, no matter how limited, theory and history of the arts and arts appreciation are meaningless. In this same context, however, all the arts and their cultures must be talked about in equal terms, although certainly not in equal strength or coverage, for to expect this is impossible.

Technology
Since the invention of television and the computer, we have been living in a world where technological innovation is becoming increasingly sophisticated and competitive, with the products of that innovation more and more readily accessible. The relationship between the live performing arts and advances in computer, video, and audio technologies is, therefore, an increasingly more significant factor in our field. Television has also had a profound effect in areas of cultural conflict and cultural assimilation, as television personalities act as role models

(both positive and negative), and as the language of TV becomes our linguistic norm.

This brief discussion of technology has one purpose: to call for fresh investigation into the medium's changing relationship to the performing arts. Technology is relevant in several significant ways: as a means of marketing and promoting arts events; as a means of educating the public about the performing arts and the diversity of artistic and cultural expressions being created and preserved; and as a means of new expression, exploiting technology by incorporating it into the artwork itself, whether for live performance on stage or for work specifically created for television, video, or radio.

Ralph Sandler and Patricia Eldred, in "Performance or Paradigm: Inspiration, Creation, and Communication in the Arts and Anthropology," explore technology as a means of expression:

> Today's performing artists overwhelm their
> audiences with sound, lights, lasers, giant video
> monitors, strobes and smoke coming from millions
> of dollars worth of equipment. This employment of
> technological wizardry is sometimes used to cover up
> artistic inadequacies. More often, however, artists
> are using computers, video, lasers, etc. in very
> creative ways, allowing them to introduce images
> and sounds that were previously impossible to create
> on stage in a live performance. Laurie Anderson,
> using a special piece of sound equipment, is able to
> manipulate the tone, timbre and volume of her voice
> by turning a dial. Philip Glass, David Henry
> Hwang, and Jerome Serlin's 1000 Airplanes on the
> Roof, which premiered in an airplane hangar in
> Vienna, used multiple slide projections to produce
> the illusion of three-dimensional spaces, changeable
> at the touch of a button. Composers and
> performance artists are becoming more comfortable
> with advances in technology and are perceiving the
> virtually limitless possibilities of marrying the
> scientific and aesthetic.

The future of taped and live performance is still in
the making. For some, that future looks grim. Suzanne
Weil, in her perspective paper, "The Media and Its Ramifi-
cations for the Future of the Live Performing Arts," fore-
sees

> *meager interaction, very little cross-nurturing, more*
> *stagnation than growth. In fact, I see media and I*
> *see live performing arts (with a few notable*
> *exceptions) both in a dreary state, looking at each*
> *other somewhat suspiciously and competitively.*

Nor does Weil believe that public TV will be a
cure-all. "Use public television" she advises, "but don't
expect it to take the lead in ideas, enthusiasm, and/or
money."

On the other hand, "Alive from Off Center," produced at the Walker Art Center, is an excellent example of
the collaboration that can occur when an innovative
presenter, a creative television producer, and outstanding
contemporary artists work together with this new technology. As John Schott, producer of "Alive from Off Center," describes it, video technology is just another tool
that has yet to be fully utilized.

Virtually everyone acknowledges that the opportunities for creativity in all of these areas, and in their
imaginative combination, are as limitless as our willingness to explore them. Artists have been well ahead of
presenters and broadcasters in applying television to performance, and vice-versa. Working primarily in video,
and often manipulating the technology so that it becomes an integral part of the work, these artists have
recast video cassette distributors and broadcasters as living room presenters. Given the proliferation of VCRs and
video cassette outlets, increased viewing of both cable
and video, and the development of high-definition TV,
more people are likely to spend more time watching
television, and more artists will want to work with the
medium.

Radio also offers untapped and unrealized potential. For example, the use of radio was expanded by the

New York City Department of Cultural Affairs through the introduction of live performances by lesser-known music groups on a commercial station. The department's commissioner advocated this arrangement as a way of getting wider exposure for the groups and broadening audience awareness of the artistic resources to be found in their city.

If presenters and local broadcasters spend their time "looking suspiciously" at one another, they will only leave themselves standing while artists and their audiences move on. Outright curiosity and a little creativity could go a long way toward making the artist-presenter-broadcaster combination "the start of a beautiful friendship."

Why do artists leave the comfort of their homes and studios to venture out on the road, touring to familiar and unfamiliar places? Perspective paper writer Rebecca Lewis, in "The Perfect Presenter," writes that when artists were asked why they tour, they responded

> *as though they had been asked why they breathe, answering: in order to live, in order to work, in order to see one's work performed, to work out ideas, to season work, for the magic of communication with an audience, and as an impetus for the creation of new work. In the words of one choreographer, "If dance doesn't tour, it doesn't exist."*

Touring is an essential part of our cultural ecosystem. It provides the means of exposure to a wide range of works and disciplines. It supports artists and brings them together with new audiences. It provides artists with a means to create or recreate a work of art. It gives audiences an important point of contact with professional artists and the art they create or interpret. And it feeds the local artistic community, entertaining audiences with established classics that educate and enrich, as well as introducing new works, different ideas and fresh interpretations.

Issues of access are very much bound up in any discussion of touring, given the importance of creating opportunities for audiences throughout the United States to experience the best and most diverse artists and artworks as regularly as possible. Some would say that creating good art and making it widely accessible are in opposition. A decade ago, this discussion was framed in loaded terms like "elitism" and "populism." But to persist in seeing a conflict between quality and access is to hold a narrow view of both public obligation and the arts.

Because of their relative isolation, access to a broad spectrum of touring artists and companies is an especially urgent issue for rural and small communities. Equally urgent is the issue of self-determination, recognizing that those communities should decide what is appropriate for them rather than being told by outside agencies.

Touring is particularly influential because it can create a critical mass of local audience support, potentially creating resident companies in a progression of local interest: as audiences become more familiar with, and interested in, work that they see on tour, they are more apt to create a demand for resident companies. Audiences are also more likely to support those companies through attendance, donations, and volunteer service.

This progression might have more impact on future audiences if more touring reflected the cultural traditions of new immigrant communities and long-established non-white populations. Touring that responds to and reflects our cultural diversity should be supported, and the development of venues, presenters, and resident companies for such work should be encouraged.

Touring culturally specific work will be even more challenging if, as our society becomes more diverse, higher costs result in the establishment of fewer resident companies. A shortage of resident performing companies already exists in many cultural communities, and some predict that resources even for the largest and wealthiest companies will shrink. Presenting has always been an expensive proposition, though it is less expensive in many communities to present work on tour than to provide ongoing support for resident companies. Our goal must be to provide adequate support for artists and companies both at home and on the road. Now, in an atmosphere of economic constraint, our field must commit new human and financial resources to touring the widest range of work on the broadest possible scale.

The Touring Artist

When it functions as it should, touring provides financial and creative support for artists and offers broad access to their work. Like the field as a whole, touring artists are a diverse group working in many ways and forms. They include artists who perform alone or in ensembles; artists who represent any discipline and any style of work within that discipline; artists for whom touring is the primary enterprise and those for whom it is secondary or even tertiary, although not always by design. In this latter category are many artists who are poorly compensated and must earn a living at something else throughout the week in order to tour on weekends.

One problem that touring artists face has been the narrow definition of "a tour." In the past, a tour was regarded as a certain number of consecutive engagements occurring in an organized route at a considerable distance from home. In fact, touring takes other forms as well. For example, it includes traveling away from home but staying in one place, where the artist and presenter work closely together over a long period of time. Touring may also be described as a hub-and-spoke arrangement in which an artist "lives" at the presenter's hub facility and visits other presenters in a close geographic area. Run-outs from a company's home base may also constitute touring.

In short, a restrictive definition of touring is of little value in determining how artists should be supported. Emphasis must be on the artist and his or her needs in taking the art on the road. Attaching geographic or mileage limitations to such support should be avoided if possible.

For the artist, touring offers both the potential for abundant opportunity and a grueling routine. Often, touring inhibits or prevents the creation and rehearsal of new work. Extremes and contrasts pervade almost everything about it. A "new" artist or company may be eager to go on the road for the experience; yet presenters who could enable that tour to happen are uninterested in or unfamiliar with the artist or work, can't afford it without subsidy, or are unwilling to commit resources to take a risk. On the other hand, artists or companies that have toured extensively for years may be exhausted by the experience and would do anything to build longer seasons at home, sometimes just as their popularity is rising and presenters are eager to engage them.

Part of the grind of the road is that many tours have become a sequence of one-night stands. Where residencies were once common, they are now much more rare. The result is that in many places, artists lose the opportunity to create a fuller educational context for their work or to benefit from audience reaction to it. These circumstances are attributable in part to funding limitations that force artists and presenters, like everyone else, to be in constant pursuit of earned income.

Artists are of two minds. Some are resentful of touring because it robs them of time in the studio. Touring is antithetical to "making work," they say, and it no longer buys the creative time they need. Others feel differently: they are fed creatively by their experiences on the road and by their interaction with other cultures and people; these influences may, in turn, result in new artforms, styles, and works.

When artists tour, the works they perform become part of the overall repertory of their group. If they have been on the road for a long time, they often want to build a less familiar, more challenging repertory that feeds them creatively. But presenters, who must be sensitive to their own financial needs, may lag behind. Some artists complain that presenters want only safe and familiar material that they can be assured of selling. Often this may lead to artistic stagnation for touring artists and companies, because they cannot successfully tour with repertory that is too adventurous if presenters are unwilling to take risks and expose audiences to unfamiliar material.

Artists also speak of the "maturing" process that occurs when they are challenged — for example, by an increased scale of production and size of company. Such work is often the result of a close collaborative relationship between the artist who makes it, the presenter who commissions it, and the artist manager who raises support for it in the form of finding the space and time to perfect and produce the work. Unfortunately, work created on a large scale for a particular house often has a very limited number of places to tour, since few houses can accommodate the size, complexity, or cost of these large productions. Whatever the scale of the work, touring artists are frequently discouraged by the technical limitations of the spaces they encounter. The zest to create, even given the necessary tools, can't always be sustained or fulfilled. All parties in the touring process — artists, managers, presenters, funders, and audiences — must acknowledge that touring necessitates compromise.

The Task Force observed that many artists seem to have only the most minimal expectations of presenters: a place to sleep, a place to work, and time enough to do both. Perhaps this is because artists have learned that, too often, this is all they can expect. In the effort to encourage, promote, and broaden touring, presenters must take the initiative in providing artists with more than the barest necessities. In addition to meeting physical and logistical needs, presenters should commit resources to help artists realize programs of unusual interest, develop new works, or simply find time to create. Money is not always the issue or the response. For example, presenters can provide both touring and local artists with studio or rehearsal time in their facilities when they are dark. The Task Force witnessed close presenter-artist relationships most frequently in those disciplines, such as dance and chamber music, where artists rely primarily on tours for their income and performance opportunities. Not surprisingly, it is here that the links between presenters and the discipline networks are strongest.

Thus, touring can become more than a string of unrelated one-night performances. Both the presenter and the artist have the opportunity to develop long-term commitments that help create context for the art and involve the community more completely. The new Dance on Tour program of the NEA, for example, holds the potential of fostering cooperative relationships among the partners in the process. But this can only happen when artist, presenter, and manager work together and serve as resources to one another in the service of some larger artistic vision and community purpose.

Commissioning offers one important way for the relationship between the artist and the presenter to deepen, providing the artist with resources solely for the purpose of making new work. The circumstances under which that work is made will vary: on site, for example, in the presence of local artists and others, in a facility provided by the presenter; or initiated in the artist's home studio, after which it is performed, perfected, or produced elsewhere. The artist may also be a partner in the commissioning process by helping to raise funds to underwrite a new work. Support for the process of creating work within the touring context should be encouraged, while at the same time the fragility of that process should be recognized.

Merce Cunningham, in his discussion with Art Becofsky, states that multi-year, long-term commitments in the form of commissioning help him "keep a company in an honorable fashion."

> *I think it's a very good trend. It's a relief. I can think about other things. I can work in a different way. I know there will be opportunities. I know that, from my own point of view, I would always go on making something. But with these commitments, I can gear myself in a different way. And of course it's wonderful to be able to commit to dancers that they'll be able to eat!*

Whether we look at Merce Cunningham Dance Company's ongoing relationship with presenters in Minneapolis and Austin, Hancher Auditorium's relationship with the Joffrey Ballet, or Cornell University's relationship with actor/writer John O'Neal, all are examples of how a commitment can grow among people who care about each other's work.

Surely one antidote to the grind of the road is to be found in these nurturing relationships. They result in new work, new experiences for audiences, a new understanding among the partners in the presenting process, and new creative opportunities. In effect, they can be the ultimate expression of our mutuality of purpose.

6 EQUITY, DIVERSITY, AND INTERNATIONAL PRESENTATION

Cultural equity in presenting and touring the performing arts was probably the most compelling and challenging subject addressed by the Task Force. It would have been impossible to conduct a credible and comprehensive national forum, or to locate presenting and touring in their larger cultural context, without such discussion. Cultural equity acknowledges that every culture has worth and that its worth must be recognized, expressed, presented, and supported. Achieving cultural equity is an undertaking of the highest priority in which our field, along with the nation, must join. Cultural equity becomes a matter of utmost urgency when, as one Task Force member lamented, "the sands of our cultures are slipping through our fingers."

Equity is not a one-dimensional issue; it applies to many communities. Robert Garfias articulates the principle that drove the Task Force's discussions when he writes, "Cultural diversity must be seen as the strength of this nation rather than as one of its difficulties." Reymund Paredes, a scholar who has considered this question, suggests that what we are seeking in this country is a set of definitions that change the white male paradigm of an American. In its place may emerge a new *set* of paradigms, not just one, that further empower different cultural groups to speak for themselves and that foster cross-cultural fertilization without assimilation, appropriation, or suppression.

This profound shift in the way we define American culture and American art has tremendous implications for public and private funding agencies and nonprofit presenting organizations. Demographic change is already rewriting the story of community dynamics and institutional responsibility. As power shifts (and it will, despite tremendous resistance), the present economic, political, and cultural stories must be rewritten to reflect new realities.

The art we sustain and how we sustain it, the artists on our stages, and the audiences in our halls must attest to the equity amid diversity that is our goal. This comes at a time when all arts organizations, including many presenting organizations, are struggling to survive. The support structures for many organizations are stretched to capacity, making it nearly impossible to do what they have always been doing, let alone more. But this is our challenge: to keep all of our arts and cultural organizations strong while expanding the art, artists, and cultural expressions they present and the audiences they reach. This includes recognizing, helping to establish, and supporting organizations dedicated to culturally specific work and artists of color.

We must also consider the language used generally in this country and in our field to discuss the issues of cultural equity, diversity, and exchange. The Task Force sometimes found that two people talking about the same matters — using outdated language or language that carried conflicting meanings and personal associations — scarcely understood one another. Terms like "multicultural," "ethnic," and "minority" are often code words for African American, Asian, Latino, and Native American. Such language blurs discussions of race and culture, making agreement difficult; culture does not equal race, and the "minority" population in some places in the United States is white.

Diversity

Central to almost all of the Task Force's discussions were issues of collaboration and control. For effective collaboration to occur, those involved must be equals in decision making. Each party has to bring something to the table if all are to walk away satisfied that they have gained. But as Robert Garfias cautions, "having the right folks around the table is, however, only the first step. There must also be a willingness to hear what they are saying, and this usually requires much, much more than just hearing the words."

The Task Force heard many attempts at collaboration characterized as imbalanced and opportunistic — efforts to appropriate the "weaker" organization's mailing list and audience — even if they were not intended as such. Task Force members recognized that collaboration is often a difficult undertaking, one that requires time, patience, practice, and mutual respect. The pitfalls are many. Pearl Cleage, in her perspective paper, "How Can We Sing the Lord's Song in a Strange Land?", powerfully illustrates how a joint venture can go wrong — in this case, between an independent black theatre company and a large white producing organization. The companies collaborated on a gospel production and the collaboration was meant to initiate an "exchange of ideas and resources at every level," including long-term fundraising, marketing, promotion, and audience development.

But many months later, it had become clear that "the reality was much grittier" than this dream. Cleage continues:

> About one-half hour into the show, a middle-aged black man in the third row, center section, leaped to his feet and "got happy." He threw his head back and whooped. He stiffened his body and his eyes rolled back. He jerked his arms and rocked his head and stamped his feet and shouted his praises to his God.
>
> Well, now, I thought, watching his energy flowing toward the stage and feeling the performers feeding off that energy, that response, that willingness to participate in the ritual that is so much a part of African American religious and secular and theatrical ceremony. Now, I thought, we're getting somewhere.
>
> The thought barely had time to register fully before I noticed three grim-faced ushers hurrying toward the man, who was now standing in the center aisle clapping and calling encouragement to the stage congregation. The three white ushers... surrounded the man quickly, one at each arm and one picking up his hat and coat from his seat; and as he looked around in embarrassed confusion, they hustled him unceremoniously down the middle aisle and out of the door.
>
> I realized in horror that they had put the man out

for disrupting the play...

Cleage goes on to provide her personal perspective:

*I felt ashamed of my part in bringing this man to
this place to be publicly humiliated for obeying
cultural commands that were as deeply a part of
him as the color of his skin. What were we doing
there anyway, him and me,* trying to sing the
Lord's song in a strange land?

One Task Force member, commenting on this
story, described it as a situation in which *everyone* made
mistakes except the man who stood up. Clearly the large
theatre was unprepared for that man's response and
handled it inappropriately. Clearly there was insufficient
communication between the companies about what to
expect from the audience and how to react. Collaborative
projects that bring together differing, and potentially
conflicting, traditions and customs require extensive,
ongoing and open dialogue among all parties. Had that
communication occurred in this case, the outcome might
have been very different.

"We must recognize," another member concluded,
"that in a changing society, given the challenges and
sometimes the awkwardness of our efforts at collaboration, we are *all* 'trying to sing the Lord's song in a strange
land.'"

Pregones, a professional community-based ensemble that presents Latin American and Puerto Rican
theatre, has also confronted the issue of cross-cultural
collaboration. In her paper, Caron Atlas describes their
approach to it:

*[Pregones has] found that many of the traditional
arts presenters who have the resources to bring them
are not connected, or even accessible to, the
communities the company most wants to reach. So
they have developed a residency program which
establishes links, before the tour, with local tenant*

groups, culturally active service agencies, and civil rights groups. Their performances become part of an ongoing process — an activist campaign, festival, or cultural program — within the community. Writes company member Alvan Colon, "Latino theatre cannot be used as bait for 'outreach' to fill mainstream theaters. When our theater is presented as an exotic cultural product, or when it is watered down to make it palatable to Anglo audiences, it results in a deformed or distorted view of our culture."

Follow the thread of cultural equity, definition, language, and collaboration, and one comes to the issue of control. For people from any culture, this means having control of their own cultural symbols and images and exercising that control.

Why is this necessary? The answer is that when the content of one culture is left solely to another to express, without any consultation with that culture's community, then the result is usually distorted, unintentionally or by design. This outcome is even more likely — and more threatening — if the two cultures are at odds: haves and have-nots, majority and minority, victor and vanquished. This is particularly true because the art coming from people of color and culturally specific communities often challenges the dominant political system and values and the prevailing aesthetic criteria.

In short, no culture can survive intact if its interpretation and transmission are controlled by people outside the culture. Culturally specific organizations are more likely to have the best knowledge about indigenous artforms and artists, and about the communities from which both come. Yet there has been insufficient support for culturally specific presenting organizations. With great perseverance, communities have been able to develop presenting organizations such as the Guadalupe Cultural Arts Center in San Antonio, the Afro-American Cultural Center in Charlotte, North Carolina, the Native American Center for the Living Arts in Niagara Falls, the

Caribbean Cultural Center in New York City, and the
Japanese American Cultural and Community Center in
Los Angeles. Other, similar organizations need to be created and sustained throughout the country. These
organizations can create environments more "sympathetic" to the art and artists being presented and nurture
artists in significant ways. Two-thousand-seat concert
halls house the symphonies, and those with orchestra
pits accommodate the operas. But artforms from many
other traditions often require different spaces, outdoor
environments, or more intimate settings.

This is not to say that presenters using 2,000-seat
halls are relieved of the responsibility to diversify their
programs. For example, innovative uses of large halls for
festivals that embrace the diversity of a community's
population can provide a collaborative link between an
"established" concert hall and a broadened constituency.
Such use can also help to foster a more open climate for
discourse within a community, stemming not from isolation and distrust but rather from access and respect.

Because culturally specific presenting organizations are so varied, because they may not "look like" (nor
want to look like) existing presenting and touring organizations, many of them have difficulty securing recognition and support outside of their communities. This may
be the case despite a strong track record of stability,
experience, and close community ties. When they represent newly arrived immigrants or poorer groups, their
resources may be especially limited; community support
is likely to go first to social service and health needs.
Sometimes these organizations are based in rural areas of
the country where, in addition to contending with pov-
erty, they must overcome the disadvantage of a small
population spread over a large area with inadequate trans-
portation and communication networks.

It is imperative that public and private funding
sources carefully consider the needs of organizations of
color and those presenting culturally specific work by
conducting an extensive review of their own grantmak-
ing policies to determine if they are equitable. These

organizations look different because they are often part of a larger organization for which presenting is only one of many functions. More funds and other resources — such as space, equipment and special expertise — must be generated if the cultures, expressions, and traditions that these organizations represent are not to suffer.

The fact that there was strong support within the Task Force for the work of culturally specific presenting organizations does not mean that other presenters are exempted from building more diverse programs, a wider audience base, and more equitable support systems. Toward this end, serious and carefully thought-out efforts to collaborate with organizations of color and culturally specific organizations — where their expertise is valued, respected, listened to, and acted upon — represent a challenging agenda for the future.

For organizations in rural and small communities, issues of control and self-determination are also paramount. The needs of rural and small communities are often overlooked in arts policy deliberations, or are addressed as though applying a metropolitan perspective to the entire United States. Specific skill development is needed to encourage effective presenting in the rural/ small context. Innovative and flexible funding programs could provide greater access to the arts for this underserved constituency, as could presenter-based touring programs designed specifically for rural and small communities. Sharing the cultural gifts and artistic talent of these communities with more urban areas must be part of any program of recognition and support.

Issues of diversity and equity are not exclusive to matters of race and ethnicity. We are all deprived if an artist's work is suppressed because of that artist's gender or sexual preference. This is a particularly timely concern in presenting the work of gay and lesbian artists, whose contributions to American art have been so important. As their work becomes more urgent and more visible, it has provoked a backlash in some quarters that would censor these artists and those who present them. Our clear responsibility as a field is to stand together and to encourage and support these artists, their work, and the presenting organizations that give them a home. This responsibility is even more compelling as more works confront the AIDS epidemic. Although AIDS is not limited to the gay community, the early affliction of large numbers of gay people has prompted and shaped many powerful works of art. We must all have the opportunity to experience these works as, tragically, AIDS steadily becomes a broader American experience.

In effect, we have an opportunity to help build an American society and an American art that draw their vitality and spirit from our country's remarkable diversity. But as Robert Garfias points out, "Our cultural and educational institutions will have to do much less well-intentioned doing *for* the other Americans and much more doing *with* them if the effects of long years of indifference and hostility are now to be overcome."

International Presentation

In considering the subject of international presentation, the Task Force heard the echo of issues that permeated every other discussion: access, context, equity, representation, education, support, and advocacy. With international presentation, however, the issues take on the added dimension of government regulation of the immigration and visa-granting process. In this arena, our field has had very little impact.

In order for us to understand our place as Americans in the world, we must have access to the cultural expressions of other countries. Just as it is important for residents of New York City to have the opportunity to experience Queen Ida and the Bon Temps Zydeco Band, or for those of San Francisco to experience Ballet Hispanico, it is equally important to attend performances of the Frankfurt Ballet or the National Dance Company of Senegal. Neither geographical nor political barriers should prevent audiences from encountering the best and most varied of the performing arts and artists from throughout the world. Overcoming these barriers — both here and abroad — requires curiosity, patience, financial resources, the determination to contend with government regulations, and the tenacity to surmount differences in language and customs.

Some of the international work that is brought to the United States is presenter-generated and takes place outside the structure of the commercial managements. Sometimes its presentation is motivated by a simple interest in seeing and hearing the great performers and ensembles of the world. Sometimes it is motivated by a deep commitment on the part of culturally specific organizations to the most authentic expressions of their own heritages. A presenter who usually offers European-derived works may want to provide works from another country for the benefit of certain culturally specific communities within his or her area, or to expose audiences generally to a wide range of other works in order to expand their understanding of world cultures. In all of these ways, artists and works of art must be imported to celebrate living cultures rather than to profit from exotica. Context is also a factor in considering the appropriate venues for international work, just as it is in presenting the work of any culture or period.

Considerations of cultural journalism, education, and the appropriateness of performance facilities apply also to the presentation of artists from foreign countries. It is even more crucial that the presenter do whatever is necessary to learn about these artists and artworks and about the cultural contexts in which they belong. To accomplish this, a dialogue must be initiated with local residents who come from and understand the cultures being presented, and this must be done far in advance of performance. Part of the challenge is to find a way to present foreign artists in an environment that may be unaccustomed to their presence, and to overcome audience intimidation and hostility.

Presenters must also realize that foreign artists will need assistance in making the transition to a different culture. All of the issues that are related to the responsibilities of presenters to American touring artists become even more meaningful when the artists are international

guests. If the presenter is in a diplomatic relationship
with a foreign government, then he or she is even more
challenged to deal successfully with international poli-
tics, currency exchange, work permits, and other related
issues.

There was clear consensus in the Task Force that
the United States government has undervalued and un-
derfunded the arts as a component of international relations. What is needed in response is for the arts community to find new, more persuasive ways to make the case
for government support for both importing and export-
ing works of art.

Our Canadian colleagues have recognized the
value of the arts as a tool for diplomacy, trade, and
international exchange. There the argument for government support, developed by the staff of the Cultural
Relations Branch of the Department of External Affairs
(the Canadian equivalent of our State Department) was
framed in terms of the economic benefit that the arts can
bring by enhancing international trade. This argument
was directed internally, at the department itself, which
then embraced the principles of international cultural
relations as an economic benefit and as part of its foreign
policy. The result was a doubling of government funding
over a four-year period, beginning in 1986, for the export
of Canadian artists abroad as well as the import of artists
to Canada.

This same case might be made in the United
States. Another pragmatic approach might be to allocate
part of the State Department's enormous foreign aid budget
to a "percent-for-culture" program. This would entail
earmarking a fraction of the total allocation to each
foreign country to facilitate cultural exchange in both
directions.

Still another option, requiring a level of advocacy
which has not yet been demonstrated, would be to lobby
for an allocation to the National Endowment for the Arts
of an additional 25 percent of its budget. These added
funds would be used to support the presentation and
dissemination of international and culturally diverse art-

ists and artforms, in a program overseen by a deputy chair of the Endowment named for this purpose. The Endowment could then be an authority and resource on related matters, advising the United States Information Agency and the Immigration and Naturalization Service, among others, on policies and procedures that affect international presenting and touring.

In addition to adequate funding, appropriate technical assistance is needed to teach presenters how to help artists overcome the barriers to international exchange. This includes advocating for the elimination of those barriers through legislation and administrative procedures. Very often, everyone involved in a particular international exchange project is doing so for the first time. Technical assistance — including informational handbooks and seminars — would be valuable.

Finally, our field could take the initiative in this area with a forum to help establish an agenda for international exchange, appropriate educational programs for presenters, information services covering foreign artists and companies, and an expanded dialogue with artists' unions in order to address their concerns about the effects of international exchange on their members.

7   EXTERNAL SUPPORT STRUCTURES

External support structures assist in the exchange
between artist and audience and enhance a presenting organization's ability to carry out its mission. They include
artist managers; service organizations; the funding and
other support mechanisms of local and state arts agencies,
regional organizations, the National Endowment for the
Arts, private foundations, corporations; and the system of
booking and touring.

Booking Conferences

Both presenters and managers have expressed
their concern that traditional booking conferences suffer
from a number of problems. First, they tend to place the
artist outside the relationship between the manager and
presenter, where he or she is more susceptible to being
treated as incidental. Second, they create a relationship
defined almost entirely by the economic transaction rather
than the artistic one. Third, they display artworks and
artists much like ready-to-wear garments, to be sold off
the rack without any true consideration of the special
needs and opportunities that each artist and presenter
represents, or of the possibilities that occur when they
work together. And fourth, because they require travel,
staffing, and expense, booking conferences might be
viewed as excluding many individuals and smaller arts
organizations. As presently configured, these conferences
do not represent the breadth and diversity of our arts
communities.

Many veterans of booking conferences talk about
their value despite these commercial trappings. They offer
a relatively affordable opportunity for face-to-face communication, enabling those who are interested in artists
and artforms to exchange ideas and talk about who and
what they have recently seen and heard. Not surprisingly,
the most effective conferences incorporate performances
and provide strong professional development opportunities for presenters, artists, and managers.

The Task Force has learned a great deal from its
own experience of bringing together a widely diverse
group of people to discuss issues. In a similar way, oppor-

tunities must be created at booking conferences for the partners in the presenting and touring process to meet and discuss projects and ideas outside of the sales atmosphere of the resource room. Indeed, if we begin to view conferences as gatherings of the field rather than solely as opportunities for commerce, they will become much more effective.

Artist Managers

The overriding role of the artist manager is to build the careers and protect the business interests of the artists they represent. In the best of circumstances, managers are completely conversant with their artists and companies and the work they create and perform. These managers serve as an informational resource and a partner in the presenting and touring process.

Just as presenter roles are changing, so too are the roles of manager. Many managers are acting as catalysts for new relationships that include the artists they represent, in some instances providing the initial leadership needed to define and implement collaborative projects. It is not uncommon for managers to write grant applications for artists, or to fundraise in the private and corporate sector to help an artist or company they represent realize some specific project or acquire ongoing support. We also see some managers taking on multiple roles, sometimes including presenting. For example, Jon Aaron of Aaron Concert Management in Boston presents a recital and chamber music series in addition to running his own artist management firm. Jedediah Wheeler of International Production Associates has been representing contemporary performing artists as well as acting as presenter and producer for Lincoln Center's Serious Fun program.

Conversely, some presenters have taken on the additional responsibilities of representing artists, booking, and managing tours. One example is the Caribbean Cultural Center's "Under One Sun" tour, offering some of the African and Caribbean music and dance groups it has presented in its own concerts over the past twelve years.

The Japanese American Cultural and Community Center in Los Angeles took on this added role as well when, in 1988, it managed a United States tour of Bunraku: The National Puppet Theatre of Japan.

To regard managers solely as salespeople does them a serious disservice. Many artist managers see more performances than most presenters, have a comprehensive knowledge of the national touring scene, and have been (or are) artists themselves. Clearly, we need to view them as significant resources for our field.

Service Organizations

Service organizations that affect the presenting field have grown in size and number in recent years. They include the Association of Performing Arts Presenters, the International Society of Performing Arts Administrators, Western Alliance of Arts Administrators, Chamber Music America, Dance U.S.A., the National Jazz Service Organization, The Association of American Cultures and others.

Service organizations have different characteristics and serve different kinds of needs. Some are discipline-specific, others are geographically oriented. In general, they have been effective vehicles for encouraging communication about issues and needs among like-minded people. Now they must begin to serve as a bridge to others outside of their immediate constituency, in both continuing and expanding the dialogue that the field has initiated through the Task Force. It will be in the best interests of the arts for discipline-based service organizations to address presenter issues in order to assure that the needs and concerns of their constituents are clear to presenters. One important step is to encourage and support relationships in which institutions and individuals seek one another out because of their common interest in an idea or artist, rather than for geographic proximity. And in cooperation with funders and policy makers, service organizations can collect data on their constituents to contribute to a comprehensive picture of what the field of presenting looks like.

State Arts Agencies and
Regional Organizations

An increasing number of state arts agencies and regional organizations are developing imaginative programs to fill gaps and meet needs in presenting and touring in their areas. In the process, more of them are nurturing their unique artist resources and helping to provide a base of support for local artists.

Because broad geographical participation in the arts is a priority of most state arts agencies, their staffs are often in regular communication with numerous presenters. Thus, state arts agencies are well-positioned to call meetings of presenters and others, to begin a dialogue on issues raised in this document, and to develop concrete ways of implementing recommendations that are suitable for them.

Technical assistance programs already available in most state arts agencies should be expanded to include presenters, if this is not already the case. Technical assistance could take the form of travel funds to see new, unfamiliar, or culturally diverse work; seminars at which work is seen and discussed in its fullest cultural context; and training in collaborative ventures among different kinds of presenters. Service organizations should be natural partners in these programs.

By and large, state arts agencies/regional organizations and presenters still maintain a grantor/grantee relationship, rather than working together as partners in a larger process. Achieving more complex, more productive, and less linear relationships is part of the challenge for all.

Although state arts agencies and regional organizations have much in common, regional organizations are distinct and can serve other purposes. Because they are not constrained by the procedures and regulations that are typically part of governmental operations, they have great maneuverability and flexibility. Thus, regional organizations could become the places where some of the most creative and innovative programs are implemented in the future.

Funding

When presenters do their jobs well — when mutuality of purpose, engagement with artists and community, activism, and artistic vision characterize their work — it follows that adequate funding should be the rule, not the exception. Guidelines for support to presenters should encourage these outcomes so that funding becomes an integral part of the larger support structure, not just cash, and our field should be consulted as these guidelines are developed.

The discipline-based programs at the National Endowment for the Arts, in addition to having funding panels, also have panels for planning and policy making in their respective fields. But because funding for presenting organizations is dispersed throughout the programs at the NEA rather than being located in one program dedicated solely to their needs, these additional resources have been unavailable to them. It is time to create a discrete presenting organizations program at the NEA both for policy development and planning, and to marshal increased levels of funding for this important and highly diverse field.

Project support provides a mechanism for instilling change, sparking growth, and directing the field. Operating support recognizes a history of consistent presentation that meets a high level of artistry, shows developed and sustained relationships with a presenter's communities, and reflects sound management. Both types of funding have been available to producing companies. Though some regional organizations and state arts agencies offer support for marketing, and some state arts agencies provide operational support, funding for presenting has generally been limited to project or fee support. As a result, ongoing operations of presenting organizations suffer. Now, in recognition of the artistic and cultural influence of presenting organizations, operational support must be more of an option for them as well.

As a group, presenters have been less effective than many of their colleagues in the arts at developing contributed income sources, but noteworthy in their ability to generate earned income. Only recently has the field become more knowledgeable about, and active in, seeking contributions. Though presenting organizations often lack the powerful boards of directors or structural trappings that attract major support, they have the advantage of being able to devote a higher proportion of their budgets directly to artist fees rather than to the overhead that a large bureaucracy requires. As the competition for funds increases, this agility and mission-driven cost-effectiveness become a clear asset. In our rapidly changing society, the ability of presenters to respond quickly and effectively to the changing needs of our communities warrants more recognition.

The challenge for funders in supporting culturally specific work and artists of color is to keep the granting process and guidelines as open as possible. For example, culturally specific organizations do not always fit the mold of what a 501(c)(3) arts organization looks like, requiring funders to rethink the kinds of presenting organizations they are willing to fund. Funders may have to develop different review criteria to include such organizations as churches, fraternities and sororities, unions, and human services organizations. The process of building audiences and encouraging artists both begins and ends at the local level, where the work of many of these presenters and artists can have a tremendous impact that acquires national significance.

To make their best case for support, presenters will have to demonstrate that presenting and touring are essential in the lives of artists and the vitality of the communities they serve. This is best done in conjunction with artists themselves. If presenting organizations are an integral part of their local cultural ecology, then supporting them becomes all the more vital.

Data Collection

If presenters have not been effective at making their case for increased ongoing support with public and private funding agencies, it may be in part because our field lacks the comprehensive empirical data that funding agencies often require.

Because presenting and touring are always evolving, and because a good presenter works by instinct as much as by design, quantifiable data on a large scale could provide us with a clearer sense of our field and of its development over time. Among other things, this information would help us know more about who we are in number, kind, scope, budget size, and economic impact; what disciplines we present; who our audiences are; where presenters or artists are concentrated; what trends are developing in our field; and what kinds of artists and companies are available for touring.

Comprehensive data of this kind does not now exist. Though a few studies have been conducted on specific aspects of the field — such as those conducted by the Association of Performing Arts Presenters, Mid-America Arts Alliance's *Presenting In America, The Global Niche,* researched and written by The Wolf Organization, and the *National Endowment for the Arts/National Association of State Arts Agencies Survey of Support for Touring and Presenting, 1981-1984* — none provides comprehensive information on the field which has been gathered over time for trend analysis.

Amassing this kind of information will be an important step in demonstrating our field's breadth and depth and in making the case for our needs. Because there is a correlation between reliable information from data collection and the development of funding guidelines and other policies, being able to trace what has happened and to project trends in our field are both essential. Without adequate or reliable data, we are at a disadvantage in our advocacy efforts at all levels, exposed to programs that do not reflect our field's needs or interests, less effective in addressing cultural inequities, and less equipped to anticipate and plan for the future.

A note of caution is in order. We have learned from the census takers that statistical information can have profound implications, and that the method of its collection and interpretation can result in exclusion,

control, or misrepresentation. As this document demon-
strates, the National Task Force on Presenting and Touring
the Performing Arts has envisioned much more inclusive-
ness and diversity than has previously characterized the
perception of our field. Data collection will only be useful
if it reaches beyond the traditional definitions and models
of presenting organizations to embrace a wider range of
possibilities.

The Development of Parallel Structures

As presenting and touring grow more dynamic
and more diverse, the best presenters want to be more
than just buyers of arts events, bringing those events to
their communities and selling them as products. Using
presenting as their tool, they are working to meet cultural
and community needs and to be supportive of artists both
nationally and locally. Many have found that they must
initiate direct relationships with artists, funders, and other
presenters, and create different, "parallel" structures to
meet their goals. These parallel structures are being forged
alongside existing external support structures. Some parallel structures are ad hoc, set up and then dismantled as
need requires; others will likely be around for a long time.
In both cases, players in the presenting and touring continuum are developing a variety of structures that reflect
mutuality of purpose among presenters, artists, managers,
funders, and communities. Having chosen to work in
different ways, they are inventing the structures to support their pioneering efforts.

How are these parallel structures manifesting themselves? A few examples illustrate the possibilities.

In Art Becofsky's interview with him, Merce Cunningham discusses the "'affinity relationships' among
organizations with shared missions" that have made a
long-term commitment to his work. These relationships
currently exist between the Cunningham Company and
CAL Performances at the University of California at
Berkeley, the Sharir Dance Company in Austin, Texas, and
between the company and a partnership of the Walker Art
Center and Northrop Auditorium of the University of

Minnesota. The result has been an ongoing source of support for, and interest in, both new and existing pieces, and a means for Cunningham to reach the communities in which those presenters operate.

Another example of parallel structures is the development in Kansas City of a unique relationship with the Alvin Ailey American Dance Theater. The Ailey company had been engaged in Kansas City during the 1970s by college or university presenters. In 1982, discussions developed between the Gentlemen of Distinction, a black service organization, and the Folly Theatre, with the aim of structuring a long-term, community-based relationship with the Ailey Company. The idea was to reach the community in a more powerful way, not just offer isolated performances attended by a small part of the the city's population.

Ailey's interest was originally piqued by his desire to create a new work about American jazz great and Kansas City native Charlie Parker. Also important was the economic need to support the company with decentralized "second homes." Following a feasibility study by Mid-America Arts Alliance, a group of community partners formed the Kansas City Friends of Alvin Aliey. This governance partnership brought together for the first time the community foundation, a culturally diverse presenter, other presenters, local government, a performing arts institution, several community social service organizations, the state arts agency, and the regional arts organization.

Over the last six years, the Ailey project has grown to include year-round activities that have been woven into the social fabric of the community. They have done much to improve race relations in Kansas City. The most recent development, Ailey Camp, was established for at-risk youths in 1989, with funds from the Gannett Foundation. The camp uses aspects of dance, such as creative expression, critical thinking, and discipline development, to effect a change in the lives of young participants.

Yet another example of support structures in the service of new opportunities is found in productions by the Negro Ensemble Company (NEC) of playwright Charles Fuller's "WE" plays, four works about Reconstruction. The project is being coordinated by Western and Southern Arts Associates of Austin, Texas, an artist management firm that represents a small number of theatre companies. A consortium of interested presenters is being developed to create programs that go beyond performance alone.

Each presenter will engage the NEC for a one-week residency that includes up to eight performances of the four "WE" plays. Plans are underway for a significant humanities component, one that will give the plays an historical context, for which a scholar and authority on Reconstruction, Professor Eric Foner of Columbia University, is serving as advisor. A "WE" newsletter has been launched to spread the word about the plays and this project.

Nor is the "WE" project the only instance in which this kind of shared vision is evident. Consortia of presenters are developing all over the country out of mutual needs and opportunities. Where once these presenter consortia formed around block booking for economies of scale, they now are coming together in "affinity relationships" around common artistic goals or for the commissioning and production of particular works of art. In addition to presenter groups, artists with common needs and concerns have developed support and touring networks. One such network is Alternate ROOTS, an organization of performing arts companies and artists in the Southeast that supports touring among its members.

Some presenter consortia are also ad hoc, without a name or formal leadership. They come together for a specific project, such as commissioning a new work by a particular artist, and then disband until the next opportunity arises. At that time, they might reassemble with the same or different players.

This is not to say that more formal presenter consortia no longer exist; they do. In many cases, their focus has shifted from block booking to other activities more related to their specific needs, such as conducting professional development programs. They are most effective when, in this way, they are able to respond to changing needs in their own environments.

Susan Farr, in her perspective paper, "The Effect and Potential of Presenter Consortia," points to the National Performance Network (NPN) as an example of a group of individuals who coalesced around common artistic goals.

> NPN has been described as a group composed of like minds — individuals who share aesthetic, social, political, and organizational goals. Their agenda is set by their common interest in art and the support of artists. Because Dance Theater Workshop, which organized NPN, has raised substantial amounts of money to support the artists presented by NPN members, the economic issues have shifted from how to reduce the artists' fees to how to use available funding most effectively to create a meaningful relationship between the artist and the community.

In the most successful parallel structures, the funder is an integral partner in the process of support and development. The result has often been projects that take chances by reaching beyond single performances to engage an entire community on a more sustained basis. Such projects — and other programs that build long-term relationships among artists, presenters, and communities — will cost much more than single-shot underwriting. But their impact can be enormous, a fact that more funders are beginning to realize.

Unfortunately, however, funding criteria are still more likely to focus on one-time performances than on the building of relationships. Funders must recognize that presenting involves more than paying artist fees. Along with fee subsidy must come additional support for such operational necessities as marketing, outreach, front of house, box office, stagehand salaries, and equipment rental.

It is crucial that funders recognize that parallel

structures are the "research and development" side of our field. Rather than view these structures as potentially threatening, funders and policy makers must leave room in their guidelines for the flexibility that will encourage their development. This will enable them to be appropriately responsive when an idea comes along that does not quite fit existing funding criteria.

Members of the Task Force observed that, at their best, established external support structures respond to changes in the field, while parallel structures spur us forward. Both are invaluable, and both must exist in order to create the dynamism that should characterize our work.

CONCLUSION:
CONTINUING THE DIALOGUE

Considering the wealth of perspectives, analyses, and relationships detailed in this report, we must clearly approach our responsibilities in presenting and touring with "new eyes." The way presenters were seen only two decades ago — and, often, the way they saw the world — is vastly different from the portraits drawn in these pages. We must, in effect, create new stories — new paradigms, enlivened histories, and envisioned futures — to embrace current realities. The old stories simply don't work anymore.

This philosophical essay challenges all of us to continue the dialogue of the Task Force in our organizations, with colleagues and others in the field of presenting and touring, and with members of our various communities. As such, this document will only be complete if it stimulates discussion and controversy and results in action. From the largest support organization to the newest artist, every individual and institution is called on to question old assumptions, re-examine ways of operating, create new relationships, engage in new dialogues, and incorporate new insights into every aspect of our work.

From the outset, it was the Task Force's hope that this document would be read, copied, passed on, and reread by everyone associated with presenting and touring: funders, board members and staff, artists, artist managers, officials in public agencies, and others. Some organizations have already begun to use this report to rewrite their mission statements; some have used it as the focus of staff and board retreats. Whatever the means, this document can help us take the measure of our activities, our approaches to presenting and touring, our mutuality of purpose, our relationships with the field and with our communities, our support of artists, and our commitment to cultural equity. This is the work we must *all* do if we are to address the challenges before us in the years ahead.

Nothing could be more challenging, more promising, and possibly more daunting. But our lives are in the arts, after all, where creativity, curiosity, and the highest standards must be our hallmarks. Over many months of discussion, the Task Force became increasingly more certain that if our field considers and responds to the ideas presented in this essay, we can have a profound impact on American society and the changes that are shaping it.

Our job, then, is to make certain that the new stories that represent our common experiences are developed as creatively as we know how, and that they touch as many people as possible. If we succeed, our lasting legacy will be the work of those most creative among us — the artists who are best able to see beneath the surface of our actions and make order of our infinite complexity.

MEMBERS OF THE NATIONAL TASK FORCE
ON PRESENTING AND TOURING
THE PERFORMING ARTS

Steering Committee

Gerald D. Yoshitomi, Chair
Japanese American Cultural
and Community Center
Los Angeles, CA

Marie Acosta-Colon
The Mexican Museum
San Francisco, CA

Art Becofsky
Cunningham Dance
Foundation
New York, NY

John Gingrich
John Gingrich Management
New York, NY

Charmaine Jefferson
Department of Cultural
Affairs
New York, NY

John Killacky
Walker Art Center
Minneapolis, MN

Susan Lipman
Chamber Music Chicago
Chicago, IL

Toby Mattox
Society for the Performing
Arts
Houston, TX

Henry Moran
Mid-America Arts Alliance
Kansas City, MO

Mary Regan
North Carolina Arts Council
Raleigh, NC

Edwin Romain
Delphin & Romain,
Duo-pianists
Carbondale, IL

Ralph Sandler
Madison Civic Center
Madison, WI

Kathy Dwyer Southern
American Association of
Museums
Washington, DC

David White
Dance Theater Workshop
New York, NY

Members of the Task Force

Jon Aaron
Aaron Concert Management,
MA

Jeremy Alliger
Dance Umbrella, MA

Ella Baff
University of California,
Berkeley

Leon Bates
Pianist, PA

Tandy Beal
Tandy Beal and Company,
CA

Wendy Bennett
The Bush Foundation, MN

Ludy Biddle
Crossroads Arts Council,
VT

Philip Bither
Flynn Theater, VT

Henry Bowers
Capital Area Arts Foundation,
NC

Ron Bowlin
University of Nebraska

Michael Braun
Mid-Atlantic Arts
Foundation, MD

Ken Brecher
Boston Children's Museum,
MA

Bonnie Brooks
Dance USA, DC

Trisha Brown
Trisha Brown Company, NY

Robert Browning
World Music Institute, NY

Phyllis Brzozowska
CityFolk, OH

Julie Buzard
New Dance Ensemble, MN

Tisa Chang
Pan Asian Repertory Theater,
NY

Wallace Chappell
University of Iowa

H. T. Chen
Chen and Dancers, NY

Paul Chin
La Pena, CA

Laurie Beth Clark
Independent artist, WI

Kenneth Clay
Kentucky Center for the Arts

Pearl Cleage
Just Us Theater Company, GA

Dudley Cocke
Roadside Theater, KY

Shelley Cohn
Arizona Commission on the
Arts

Chris Cowden
Women and Their Work, TX

Linda Cuellar
Guadalupe Cultural Arts
Center, TX

Bruce Davis
City Celebration, CA

Jacqueline Davis
University of Kansas

Chuck Davis
African American Dance
Ensemble, NC

Jane Delgado
Arts Consultant, NY

Terrance Demas
Western Alliance of Arts
Administrators, CA

Carolelinda Dickey
Pittsburgh Dance Council, PA

Alyce Dissette
Art Producers International,
Inc., NY

Michael Doucet
Beausoleil, LA

Paul Dresher
Paul Dresher Ensemble, CA

Alejandrina Drew-Shunia
El Paso Arts Resources
Department, TX

Tim Duncan
Miami City Ballet, FL

Connie Emmerich
An Die Musik, NY

Phillip Esparza
El Teatro Campesino, CA

David Fraher
Arts Midwest, MN

Herschel Freeman
Herschel Freeman Agency,
NC

Olga Garay-Ahern
Metro Dade County Cultural
Affairs Council, FL

Cynthia Gehrig
Jerome Foundation, MN

Rob Gibson
Quantum Productions, GA

Trudy Gildea
Columbus Arts Council, MS

Gerard Givnish
Painted Bride Art Center, PA

Meg Glaser
National Council for the
Traditional Arts, DC

Joseph Golden
Cultural Resources Council,
NY

Vanessa Greene
The Afro-American Cultural
Center, NC

Robert Hankins
United Arts Council, MI

Margot Harley
The Acting Company, NY

Anne Hawley
Massachusetts Council on the
Arts and Humanities

Deborah Hay
Deborah Hay Dance
Company, TX

Patrick Henry
Free Street Theater, IL

Omus Hirshbein
The 92nd Street YM-YWHA,
NY

Joan Holden
San Francisco Mime Troupe,
CA

Michael Holden
Western and Southern Arts
Associates, TX

Christopher Hunt
Pepsico Summerfare, NY

David Hyslop
St. Louis Symphony, MO

Frank Jacobson
Scottsdale Cultural Council,
AZ

**Colleen Jennings-
Roggensack**
Dartmouth College, NH

Melvyn Jernigan
St. Louis Brass Quintet, MO

Jackie Jones
Arts Council of Oklahoma
City, OK

Paul Katz
Cleveland Quartet, NY

James Kearney
State University of New York,
Purchase

Woodie King
National Black Touring
Circuit, NY

Adrian King
Southern Arts Federation, GA

Marda Kirn
Colorado Dance Festival, CO

Sarah Lawless
Denver Center Theatre
Company, CO

Wayne Lawson
Ohio Arts Council, OH

Liz Lerman
The Dance Exchange, DC

Ruby Lerner
IMAGE Film/Video Center,
GA

William Lewis
Cuyahoga Community
College, OH

Bella Lewitzky
Lewitzky Dance Company,
CA

Joan Lounsbery
Artist Series at the Pabst, WI

Mary Luft
Tigertail Productions, FL

Arnie Malina
Helena Film Society, MT

Bruce Marks
Boston Ballet, MA

Harriet Marsh Page
Marsh Series, OH

Edward Martenson
Guthrie Theater, MN

Cynthia Mayeda
Dayton-Hudson Foundation,
MN

Ian McColl
More Productions, GA

Mimi McKell
Western States Arts
Federation, NM

Joseph Melillo
Brooklyn Academy of Music,
NY

Anthony Micocci
City Center Theater, NY

David Midland
ARTPARK,. NY

Tim Miller
Tim Miller Dance Works, CA

Cora Mirikitani
Japan Society, NY

R. William Mitchell
Walton Arts Center, AR

Nobuko Miyamoto
Great Leap, Inc., CA

John Moore
Washington Project for the
Arts, DC

John Mori
Hiroshima, CA

Lorna Myers
Purdue University, IN

Darlene Neel
Lewitzky Dance Company,
CA

David O'Fallon
University of Minnesota

John O'Neal
Junebug Theater Project, LA

Janet Oetinger
University of California,
Santa Barbara

Patrick Overton
Columbia College, MO

Elena Parres
Zona de Teatro, NM

David Peacock
Department of External
Affairs, CANADA

Peter Pennekamp
National Public Radio, DC

Michael Peranteau
DiverseWorks, Inc., TX

Ira Perman
Anchorage Concert
Association, AK

Adam Pinsker
Dance St. Louis, MO

E. Arthur Prieve
University of Wisconsin

Nigel Redden
Spoleto Festival USA, SC

Charles Reinhart
American Dance Festival, NC

Martha Rhea
Salina Arts and Humanities
Council, KS

Mary Robert
Opera Omaha, NB

Pedro Rodriguez
Guadalupe Cultural Arts
Center, TX

Randall Rosenbaum
Pennsylvania Council on the
Arts

Mark Russell
Performance Space 122, NY

Barbara Schaffer-Bacon
University of Massachusetts

Dale Schatzlein
University of Minnesota

Mikki Shepard
Shepard & Goines, NJ

Holly Sidford
New England Foundation for
the Arts

Ben Sidran
Jazz pianist, WI

Cynthia Siebert
Friends of Chamber Music,
MO

Joy Silverman
Los Angeles Contemporary
Exhibitions, CA

Lenwood Sloan
Festival 2000, CA

Shelton Stanfill
Wolftrap Foundation for the
Performing Arts, VA

Robert Stearns
Wexner Center, Ohio State
University

Kent Stowell
Pacific Northwest Ballet, WA

William Strickland
Manchester Craftsmen's
Guild, PA

Philip Thomas
The Carter G. Woodson
Foundation, NJ